DESTINY RESTORATION PILLARS

And I will restore to you the years that the locust hath eaten, the cankerworm, and the caterpiller, and the palmerworm, my great army which I sent among you.

Joel 2:25

by
Franklin N. Abazie

Destiny Restoration Pillars
COPYRIGHT 2016 BY Franklin N Abazie
ISBN: 978-1-945133-13-8

All right reserved. This book or any portion thereof may not be reproduced or used in any manner whatsoever without the express written permission of the publisher, except for the use of brief quotations in a book review. All Bible quotes are from King James Version and others as noted.

Published by: F N ABAZIE PUBLISHING HOUSE—aka, Empowerment Bookstore

That I may publish with the voice of thanksgiving and tell of all thy wondrous works.
Psalms 26:7

To order additional copies, wholesales or booking call:
the Church office (973-372-7518)
or Empowerment Bookstore Hotline (973-393-8518)

Worship address:
343 Sanford Avenue, Newark, New Jersey 07106
Administrative Head Office address:
33 Schley Street Newark New Jersey 07112
Email: pastorfranknto@yahoo.com
Website www.fnabaziehealingministries.org
Publishing House: www.fnabaziepublishinghouse.org

This book is a production of F N Abazie Publishing House. A publication Arms of Miracle of God Ministries 2016.
First Edition

CONTENTS

THE MANDATE OF THE COMMISSION....................iv
ARMS OF THE COMMISSION...................................v
INTRODUCTION...vi

CHAPTER 1
How Do I Restore My Destiny?...............................1

CHAPTER 2
Recognizing Your Talent..17

CHAPTER 3
The Power of Mentorship......................................38

CHAPTER 4
Prayer of Salvation..54

CHAPTER 5
About the Author..63

THE MANDATE OF THE COMMISSION

"The moment is due to impact your world through the revival of the healing & miracle ministry of Jesus Christ of Nazareth.

"I am sending you to restore health unto thee and I will heal thee of thy wounds, said the Lord of Host."

ARMS OF THE COMMISSION

1) F N Abazie Ministries—Miracle of God Ministries (Miracle Chapel Intl)

2) F N Abazie TV Ministries: Global Television Ministry Outreach

3) F N Abazie Radio Ministries: Radio Broadcasting Outreach

4) F N Abazie Publishing House: Book Publication

5) F N Abazie Bible School: also called Word of Healing Bible School (W.O.H.B.S.)

6) F N Abazie Evangelistic Ass: Miracle of God Ministries: Global Crusade

7) Empowerment Bookstore: Book distribution

8) F N Abazie Helping Hands: Meeting the Help of the Needy Worldwide

9) F N Abazie Disaster Recovery Mission: Global Disaster Recovery

10) F N Abazie Prison Ministry: Prison Ministry For All Convicts "Second Chance"

Some of our ministry arms are awaiting the appointed time to commence.

INTRODUCTION

*Let every man abide in the same calling
wherein he was called.*
1 Corinthians 7:20

Without a second opinion, our destiny in life is proportional and directly related to where we will live, grow, work and even die. Our destiny is significant to our lifestyle, our life attainment and accomplishment in life. We must all not continue to live life just for living sake. We must consciously take the necessary steps in life to fulfil our God-ordained destiny. If you take a self-appraisal and inventory of your life, you will notice a lot has happened to you over the period of 20 to 25 years. There have been many minor challenges — but also some dramatic and drastic challenges, as well, that have influenced and shaped your life to date.

*Moreover whom he did predestinate, them he also
called: and whom he called, them he also justified: and
whom he justified, them he also glorified.*
Romans 8:30

In my opinion, there are some vital pillars in our lives, challenges that, when displaced, change the entire outcome of our life. It is my assignment to reveal by the help of the Holy Ghost those significant pillars of life. These are destiny-molding pillars that we cannot neglect nor ignore. If you must make an impact in your lifetime, these pillars must be in place to help shape your glorious destiny.

This charge I commit unto thee, son Timothy, according to the prophecies which went before on thee, that thou by them mightest war a good warfare.
1 Timothy 1:18

Most of us with great talents, blessed to be wealthy in our lifetime, have ended up merely surviving, seeking for three square meals just to stay alive.

Apostle Paul said Wherefore we would have come unto you, even I Paul, once and again; but Satan hindered us.
1 Thessalonians 2:18

Satan is the author and responsible for harassing and hindering us from fulfilling our destiny. It is my responsibility in this book to reveal to you that we must be responsible for the outcome of our lives. We must take responsibility by doing the right thing and taking the necessary right steps to confront all our fears and prevailing challenges in life.

In these great times we live in, we must not continue to apportion blame to anyone in life. If you fail in life, it is because you made yourself a failure and accepted failure as your fate. *"When Jesus saw him lie, and knew that he had been now a long time in that case, he saith unto him, Wilt thou be made whole? The impotent man answered him, Sir, I have no man, when the water is troubled, to put me into the pool: but while I am coming, another steppeth down before me."* (John 5:6-7)

This man in the above scripture blamed his circumstance on someone. He said, *"I have no man, when the water is troubled, to put me into the pool."* I am excited to let you know that as long as you read this book, you will be armed to face all your prevailing challenges with boldness, power and authority. It will really change your lifestyle and destiny.

There are things we must do in life if we are to restore our glorious destiny in Christ Jesus. Among those significant things we must acknowledge and do are recover from the lies of the devil and to confront the issues of life with the truth of the word of God. In this great manual, you will appreciate the place of dedication, determination, discipline and personal efforts.

In my opinion, everyone who applies the principles of Jesus Christ of Nazareth will walk out on the devil with ease. I discovered that most of our prevailing challenges were lack of the wisdom of God. There is nothing God is not willing to do for us, but we must be ready to accept the gift of God without repentance. Most of us easily blame the devil for our shortcomings, failures and hindrances in life. In my opinion, our problem is not the devil. We are ignorant of the truth. *"And ye shall know the truth, and the truth shall make you free."* (John 8:32)

"But dost thou love life, then do not squander time, for that is the stuff life is made of."
Benjamin Franklin

For ages, we as believers have been confronted with attacks from the secular world about our way of life. There's been a lot of criticism and prevailing challenges facing the church of Jesus Christ. This little book will change the way you think and the way you approach life. A wise man once said, "men are in seizes, but life is in stages."

It is my personal desire to see this little book make sense in your life. It is also my personal ambition for you to repent of all your sins, develop a relationship with Jesus Christ and make straight way for your path and place in eternity. May the Holy Spirit grant you revelation as you read.

Happy Reading!

And I will restore to you
the years that the locust
hath eaten, the cankerworm,
and the caterpiller,
and the palmerworm,
my great army which I
sent among you.

And ye shall eat in plenty,
and be satisfied,
and praise the name of
the Lord your God,
that hath dealt
wondrously with you:
and my people
shall never be ashamed.
Joel 2:25-26

HIS DESTINY WAS THE CROSS....

HIS PURPOSE WAS LOVE....

HIS REASON WAS YOU....

RULES OF A WINNING LIFE

In this race of life, we must first discover ourselves before others discover the talents in us. We must recognize our strength and weakness before we make certain decisions in life. You are certain to get the worst of the bargain when you exchange ideas with the wrong person. In this race of life, always make friends with those who can inspire you, those you can learn from. The Bible says, *"He that walketh with wise men shall be wise: but a companion of fools shall be destroyed."*

Try to always be able to differentiate those God planted into your life for a season and for a long term. Information and continual learning is the key to succeed in life. Always chose your friends wisely, for evil companions corrupt good manners. Remember, "he that walk with the wise shall be wise."

In the time of prosperity we recognize our friends. *"Wealth maketh many friends."* (Proverbs 19:4) But in the time of adversity, our friends know us. *"And there is a friend that sticketh closer than a brother."* (Proverbs 18:24)

Always recognize those who make you a special person in their lives. Never make people significant in your life when you are only an option to them. The less you associate with some people, the more your life will improve. Remember Abraham did not become rich until he separated from Lot, his nephew. *"And the Lord said unto Abram, after that Lot was separated from him, Lift up now thine eyes, and look from the place where thou art northward, and southward, and eastward, and westward: For all the land which thou seest, to thee will I give it, and to thy seed for ever."* (Genesis 13:14-15)

Anytime you allow mediocrity in others, it increases your mediocrity. An important attribute in successful people is their impatience with failure, negative thinking and mediocrity. As we grow in life, our association will eventually change over time.

Eventually, you will disconnect from those that failed to improve their lives and you will connect and make friends with other successful people going up higher in the race of life. Never receive counsel from unproductive, negative-thinking people, never discus your trials and challenges with those incapable of contributing to the solution or solving your problems. Always look for the best in people around you. Develop a forgiving heart, a thankful countenance and a praiseful spirit.

Always remember this: If you are going to achieve excellence in big things, you must develop the habit in little matters. Colin Powell once said, *"A dream doesn't become a reality through magic, it takes sweat, determination and hard work. There is no secret to success, it is the result of preparation, hard work, and learning from failure."*

Excellence is not an exception. It is a prevailing attitude.

F-----FALSE
E-----------EXPERIENCE
A--------------------------APPEARING
R---REAL

F-----FACELESS
E----------------ENEMY
A--------------------------AFFLICTING
R---REASONING

F-----FREQUENTLY
E-------------------EXPECTED
A--------------------------ADVERSITY
R---REALIZED

F-----FANTACIZED
E-----------------EXAGGERATION
A---------------------------------------ABOVE
R---REALITY

F-----FIERCE
E-----------EMOTION
A----------------------AROUSING
R-------------------------------RESTLESSNESS

F-----FACELESS
E----------------EXPRESSION
A--------------------------ACKNOWLEDGED
R---REPEATEDLY

F-----FAILURE
E-------------------EXPECTED
A-----------------------------------AND
R---REHEARSED

Unless we confront our fears with faith in God, we will never fulfill the will of God concerning our lives..

HEALING KEYS

1) Always carry a positive mindset, regardless of the prevailing circumstances.

2) Always tell yourself the truth before you lie about it.

3) If the truth be told, you are a branch of His blessings, the planting of the Lord.

4) Never confess that you are sick to the hearing of the member of your body.

5) Positive confession with faith yields positive results.

6) Every cures of man have no power to prevail over your life.

7) A merry heart is medicinal and health to your body.

8) Spiritual and emotional well-being is vital to happiness in life.

9) To avoid depression, never have regrets.

10) Never be anxious in life to avoid anxiety.

11) Always live today for today to be at peace with your spirit and with God.

12) You're unique because your challenges are tailored

to you only.

12) The blessing always dominates the curses any day.

13) Decisions are the wheels of life.

14) We either ride into fame or into shame.

15) Daily exercise and some reading of the Bible gurantees good health.

16) Every day is God's day. No day created by God is a disapointment.

17) Stay away from sweet stuff—they are temporary.

18) Sugar is sweet to your taste, beware! It also contributes to diabetes.

19) A good prayer life gurantees longivity.

20) People that pray in tongues do not develop mental disease.

21) Always be positive in everything.

22) Always have a mentor in life that will oppose and fight the tormentor.

23) Always have someone in life to learn from.

24) Tell everybody what you plan to do and someone will help you do it.

25) Winners fight to the last.

26) Quitters never win in life.

27) Soul winners are heirs to the kingdom of god.

28) Soul winners never lack help.

29) Soul winners are cerified with divine help.

30) God is always looking for soul winners to bless.

31) Life is a warfare and not a funfare.

32) In life you fight for all you possess.

33) No man or woman was born rich.

34) In your lifetime do something positive to impact your world.

35) Take care of your life today—you don't have one to spare.

36) Take life serious before the devil takes you down.

37) Always be cheerful at all times.

38) Regardless of the prevailing circumstances around you, your life is in the hand of God.

39) God is the super surgeon that will spiritually-surgically heal you.

40) Always expect help from above and not from abroad.

41) Man will disappoint you, but god will appoint you.

42) The joy of the lord is always our strength.

43) Spiritual height is not measured in length or breath.

44) If you go deeper with God, you will see deeper.

45) Your next level in life is full of recognition.

46) Go to where you are celebrated and not where you are tolerated.

47) Develop yourself in the area of your calling in life.

48) A lifestyle of thanks given keeps God 24/7 on duty on our behalf.

49) Develop a lifestyle of thanksgiving.

50) Thanksgiving guarantees our access to obtain the promises.

HIGHLIGHTS TO DESTINY RESTORATION

Identification

Unless we identify our problems and confront them, we will never become great in life. For most of us, our problem is not the devil but the lack of the wisdom about God. We must seek for the revelation of the wisdom of God on any prevailing issue in our lives. Oftentimes our problem is incorrect application of the things we hear, see and read. The reason why you are poor is not the devil or any witch. We must position ourselves well in life if we are to break through on every side. We must identify within ourselves our strengths and weaknesses, along with our threats and opportunities.

Until Peter identified him, he was not the rock to build the church of God that the gates of hell shall not prevail against.

He saith unto them, But whom say ye that I am? And Simon Peter answered and said, Thou art the Christ, the Son of the living God. And Jesus answered and said unto him, Blessed art thou, Simon Barjona: for flesh and blood hath not revealed it unto thee, but my Father which is in heaven. And I say also unto thee, That thou art Peter, and upon this rock I will build my church; and the gates of hell shall not prevail against it.
Matthew 16:15-18

Confronting Every Obstacle

"Whatever you cannot confront, you cannot conquer. Whatever you cannot confront has power to prevail."

It is written, *"Rise ye up, take your journey, and pass over the river Arnon: behold, I have given into thine hand Sihon the Amorite, king of Heshbon, and his land: begin to possess it, and contend with him in battle."* (Deuteronomy 2:24)

We must develop the habit of confronting all prevailing challenges facing our lives. Remember there is always a way OUT for you, there is also a way UP for you and a way FORWARD for us all in life as long as we believe in God and have faith.

Faith In God

We must develop faith in God and in ourselves if we are to succeed in our lifetime. It takes faith in God and believing in ourselves to accomplish any great task in life. For your destiny to be recovered, we must have faith in God. *"And Jesus answering saith unto them, Have faith in God."* (Mark 11:22)

Decision

The decisions you make today will determine the future you will create. Decisions are the wheel of life, we ride into fame or into shame. If you are determined to succeed, nobody can stop you in life. Decisions are so powerful that the devil fears them—especially when you have really made up your mind.

Prayer

But ye beloved, building up your selves on your most holy faith, praying in the Holy Ghost.
Jude 1:20

As believer, we must engraft prayer as a lifestyle of something we must break through in life. Our destiny depends on our spiritual life. And our spiritual life is supported by constant prayer to God.

PRAYER POINT TO FULFILL OUR CALLING AND DESTINY IN LIFE

1) My destiny must not suffer frustration, in the mighty name of Jesus.

2) I destroy any hindering spirit caging my destiny, in the name of Jesus.

3) I must breakthrough, in the mighty name of Jesus.

4) Holy Spirit grant me access, in the Name of Jesus.

5) Power of God, grant me the GRACE to live right for Jesus Christ.

6) Hand of God, deliver me from sin, in the mighty name of Jesus.

7) Fire of God, burn every sinful thoughts from my mind, in the name of Jesus.

8) I proclaim authority over every prevailing sin in my life, in Jesus' name.

9) I destroy every root of sin in my life, in Jesus' name.

10) Sin shall not have dominion over my life, in the name of Jesus.

11) Lord God, emphasize genuine repentance over my spirit man, in the name of Jesus

12) Holy Spirit, revive and rekindle your fire of revival inside of me, in the name of Jesus.

13) Power of God, hijack the controlling forces oppressing my life, in the name of Jesus.

14) Blood of Jesus, take over my life in the mighty name of Jesus.

15) O Lord, baptize me with the gift of the Holy Spirit.

16) Holy Spirit, breathe afresh upon my life, in the name of Jesus.

17) Holy Spirit take possession of my will in the Name of Jesus.

18) Holy Spirit, make yourself real to me, in the name of Jesus.

19) Lord God of heaven, open a new chapter in my life, in the name of Jesus.

REASONS WHY
WE MUST WORSHIP GOD

—HE IS OUR CREATOR—

1) We must worship Him because He is our creator.

2) We must worship Him because He is sovereign.

3) We must worship Him because we are made in His image.

4) We must worship Him because our worship attracts His presence.

5) We must worship Him for our faith in Him to grow.

6) We must worship Him to nourish and reactivate our spirit-man.

7) We must worship Him because it activates our faith in Him.

8) We must worship Him to retain the joy of the Lord.

9) We worship Him to evict depression, envy and malice.

10) We worship Him to be happy and to escape strife and hatred.

11) We worship Him to escape bitterness, stress, anger and misery.

BENEFITS OF OUR WORSHIP

1) Worship is medicinal—it heals our soul, body and spirit-man.

2) Worship is supernatural—it positions us for constant victory in life.

3) Worship is spiritual—it grants us hope and faith in Him.

4) Worship is a mystery—it keeps us on the winning side of life.

5) Worship is faithful—it encourages us to put up the fight.

6) Worship is strengthening—it reduces the size of our problem.

7) Worship is devotional—it proves our loyalty.

8) Worship is humbling—it proves our meekness before God.

9) Worship is power—it grants us access into signs and wonders.

10) Worship is divine—it accelerates divine intervention.

11) Worship is pleasing—God takes pleasure in it.

12) Worship is a treasure—it catches the attention of God.

13) Worship is rewarding—it brings God into our trials.

14) Worship is reciprocal—it provokes God to act.

15) Worship is glorifying—it magnifies God in our situation.

16) Worship is a blessing—it opens the flood gate of heaven.

17) Worship is our responsibility—it delivers us out of obscurity.

18) Worship is deliverance—it releases us out of captivity.

19) Worship is deeper—God looks for us to prove His divinity.

20) Worship is a reminder—God remembers His promises.

21) Worship is protection—we secure His protection.

22) Worship is unity—it grants us angelic help.

WHAT TO DO WHEN MIRACLES SEEM TO BE DELAYED

1. Praise God, even in times of trouble, trial and tribulations.

2. Be expectant—expect God to move beyond your wildest imagination.

3) Be willing and obedient—God looks at your obedience in times of delay.

4) Be focused—God expects us to pay relevant attention to details.

5) Do not quit—if we must emerge winners, quitting is not an option.

6) Be positive—it can only get better, so be positive.

7) Be optimistic—your case is different, so be optimistic in life.

8) Develop an "all possibilities" mentality—every limitation is within your faith.

WHAT TO DO WHEN OTHERS SEEM TO GET THEIR MIRACLES

Hope in God

If God has done something to other individuals, we must celebrate with them. It is a sign that we are next in line. Whenever we celebrate with others, we are next in line for a miracle. We must hope and have faith in God. *"I have rejoiced in the way of thy testimonies, as much as in all riches."* (Psalms 119:14) God does not look like man, because God searches the heart, we must therefore be glad to hear the testimonies of others. *"Thy testimonies also are my delight and my counselors."* (Psalms 119:24)

Have faith in God

Unless we develop strong faith and confidence in God, we will never experience our miracles. Often God will put us on a test. Unless we pass the faith test, we will never encounter God. *"God left him, to try him, that he might know all that was in his heart."* (2 Chronicles 32:31)

We must be focused

"For his anger endureth but a moment; in his favour is life: weeping may endure for a night, but joy cometh in the morning." (Psalms 30:5) *"One man said unless we focus we will end up like locust, and unless we fast we will not last."* Every time we are distracted, we miss our miracle

from God. Focus comes with dedication and discipline in life. Jesus promised us that as long as we remain faithful and focused, we will never encounter the supernatural. *"And Jesus said unto him, No man, having put his hand to the plough, and looking back, is fit for the kingdom of God."* (Luke 9:62)

WHAT TO DO WHEN THINGS GET WORSE WHILE SEEKING GOD

—Trust in God—

"Trust in the Lord with all thine heart; and lean not unto thine own understanding. In all thy ways acknowledge him, and he shall direct thy paths." (Proverbs 3:5-6) In the midst of calamity and prevailing circumstances, we must trust in God. *"Although the fig tree shall not blossom, neither shall fruit be in the vines; the labour of the olive shall fail, and the fields shall yield no meat; the flock shall be cut off from the fold, and there shall be no herd in the stalls: Yet I will rejoice in the Lord, I will joy in the God of my salvation."* (Habakkuk 3:17-18)

1. Do not be anxious—change will come at His will.
2. When the battle gets worse, the miracle gets better and bigger.
3. Whenever we are seeking God, every negative change of situation is a setup for our promotion.
4. Those who seek God are never stranded—there is always a miracle for them.

BREAKTHROUGH PRAYER POINTS

And this is the confidence that we have in him, that, if we ask any thing according to his will, he heareth us.
1 John 5:14

—Holy Spirit of God, frustrate and disappoint everyone that is against my life and family, in the name of Jesus.
—Father Lord, destroy every demonic network and trap against my progress in life, in the name of Jesus.
—Fire of God, destroy every demonic projection and curse against my life and destiny, in the name of Jesus.
—Break every spell and curse pronounced against my destiny, in the name of Jesus.
—Hand of God, cage every power militating against my rising in life, in the name of Jesus.
—Power of God, silent every voice raising a counter motion against my elevation, in the name of Jesus.
—Blood of Jesus, neutralize every spirit of Balaam hired to hinder my life, ministry and career, in the name of Jesus.
—Fire of God, break by fire every curse that I have brought into my life through ignorance and disobedience, in the name of Jesus.
—Ancient of day, destroy every power harassing my ministry, in the name of Jesus.
—Father God, deliver me from invincible forces militating against my life and destiny.

—Power of God, frustrate every coven and demonic network, designed to frustrate and hinder my success in life, in the name of Jesus.

—I dismantle every stronghold designed to imprison my talent, in the mighty name of Jesus.

—I reject every cycle of frustration, in the mighty name of Jesus.

—Power of God, paralyze every agent assigned to frustrate my life, in the name of Jesus.

—Finger of God, grant me supernatural speed against all my contenders, in the name of Jesus.

—By the blood of Jesus, I destroy every familiar spirit caging my life and career.

—Fire of God, arrest every demonic agent assigned to police my destiny and marriage.

—By the blood of Jesus, I proclaim no weapon fashioned against me shall ever prosper.

—Holy Spirit of God, break me through and forward in life, in the mighty name of Jesus.

—Mighty God, smash me and renew my strength, in the name of Jesus.

—Holy Spirit, open my eyes to see beyond the visible to the invisible, in the name of Jesus.

—Father Lord, grant me strength and power, in the name of Jesus

—O Lord, liberate my spirit to follow the leading of the Holy Spirit.

—Holy Spirit, teach me to pray through problems instead of praying about them, in the name of Jesus.

—Father Lord, deliver me from the false accusation in

life, in the name of Jesus

—By the blood of Jesus, every evil spiritual padlock and evil chain hindering my success will be roasted, in the name of Jesus.

—By the blood of Jesus, I rebuke every spirit of spiritual deafness and blindness in my life, in the name of the mighty Jesus.

—Father Lord, empower me to dominate the enemy of my destiny, in the name of Jesus.

—Jesus Christ of Nazareth, heal my infirmities, in the name of Jesus

—Lord, anoint my eyes and my ears that they may see and hear wondrous things from heaven.

—Father Lord, anoint me with power and authority to dominate all my enemies, in the name of Jesus.

—Fire of God, roast every giant rising up against my life and career.

—Holy Spirit of God, destroy all my oppressors, in the name of Jesus.

—Angels of good news, bring my good news to me, in the mighty name of Jesus.

—Every strong man holding me down, lose your hold now, in the name of Jesus.

—I nullify every demonic prediction over my life, in the name of Jesus.

—By the blood of Jesus, I flush out every polluted deposit of the enemy in my life.

—By the blood of Jesus, I paralyze every enemy of my promotion, in the name of Jesus.

—Father Lord, destroy any power tormenting my life

that is not from You.

—Holy Ghost fire, ignite the fire of revival in my life.

—By the blood of Jesus, I declare victory over every conflicting trial.

—By the blood of Jesus, I command the arrest of every demonic spirit militating against my life.

—By the blood of Jesus, I proclaim the blood of Jesus over every device of the enemy.

—By the blood of Jesus, I revoke stagnation and hardship over my life, in the name of Jesus.

—Holy Ghost fire, destroy every satanic arrangement in my life, in the name of Jesus.

CHAPTER 1

How Do I Restore My Destiny?

*And when he came to himself, he said,
How many hired servants of my father's have bread
enough and to spare, and I perish with hunger!
I will arise and go to my father, and will say unto him,
Father, I have sinned against heaven, and before thee.*
Luke 15:17-18

A lot of us born to be celebrities in our lifetime have been suffering as a result of lack of revelation of God's word. Some of us do not see greatness in ourselves. *"But ye are a chosen generation, a royal priesthood, an holy nation, a peculiar people; that ye should shew forth the praises of him who hath called you out of darkness into his marvellous light."* (1 Peter 2:9)

As a result of lack of revelation and relevant information, a lot of us complain and suffer calamities because we do not know what to do to come out of debt and trouble. For our destinies to be restored, we must first recognize that we have a glorious destiny rooted in Christ Jesus. *"We must first identify our root in Christ. Now we, brethren, as Isaac was, are the children of promise."* (Galatians 4:28) *"And if ye be Christ's, then are ye Abraham's seed, and heirs according to the promise."* (Galatians 3:29) With this truth established, we must therefore do the following:

Be Determined

Determination is the key to success. King Solomon built a house for God because he was determined. *"And Solomon determined to build an house for the name of the Lord, and an house for his kingdom."* (2 Chronicles 2:2) We must be determined to make an impact in our lifetime. God restored the life of the prodigal son only when he was determined to return to his father. *"I will arise and go to my father, and will say unto him, Father, I have sinned against heaven, and before thee."* (Luke 15:18)

Dedication

Dedication means we must love our work. If you love what you do for a living, you will do it with excitement, delight and with joy. If you are dedicated at your work, it's only a question of time when you will break through on every side.

Discipline

As soldiers of Jesus Christ, we must be disciplined to succeed in life. *"Thou therefore endure hardness, as a good soldier of Jesus Christ."* (2 Timothy 2:3) We must discipline our mind to align with our heart and hand. We must discipline our lifestyle to meet the demands of our career and future. We must be disciplined to plan our life carefully to succeed. George Washington said, *"Discipline is the soul of an army. It makes small numbers formidable; procures success to the weak, and esteem to all."*

Extra Personal Efforts

We must endeavor to make personal efforts in our lifetime. We must put in extra efforts to see supernatural results. Until we make personal sacrifice in the area of our calling, we will not be able to fulfil our calling and destiny in life.

What Are We Saying?

For us all to restore our glorious destiny in Christ Jesus, there must be a willpower inside of us to succeed in life. We must therefore be responsible by working hard—with quitting not an option—and developing the winning ways of a champion. God has called us all with a Holy calling, but we must work towards it with all our might. *"Whatsoever thy hand findeth to do, do it with thy might; for there is no work, nor device, nor knowledge, nor wisdom, in the grave, whither thou goest."* (Ecclesiastes 9:10)

In our lifetime, we must strive to make an impact, to touch lives and to fulfil the call of God upon our lives. A lot of lazy people do not want to work in their lifetime. But remember, *"For even when we were with you, this we commanded you, that if any would not work, neither should he eat."* (2 Thessalonians 3:10)

What we are advocating here is that you must find reasonable work and do it with all your strength. *"But Jesus answered them, My Father worketh hitherto, and I work."* (John 5:17) It is written, *"I must work the works of him that sent me, while it is day: the night cometh, when no man can work."* (John 9:4)

WE MUST REPENT OF OUR SINS

"Wherefore seeing we also are compassed about with so great a cloud of witnesses, let us lay aside every weight, and the sin which doth so easily beset us, and let us run with patience the race that is set before us." (Hebrews 12:1)

We must not allow sin to destroy our calling and destiny in life. We must therefore repent of any known sin in our lives before God can restore our destiny.

For sin shall not have dominion over you: for ye are not under the law, but under grace."
Romans 6:14

Every time we yield to sin, we place ourselves in captivity. We must all strive to forsake sin and do away with every evil that dents our Christian dignity. *"Know ye not, that to whom ye yield yourselves servants to obey, his servants ye are to whom ye obey; whether of sin unto death, or of obedience unto righteousness?"* (Romans 6:16)

It is written, *"Be not overcome of evil, but overcome evil with good."* (Romans 12:21) We must all repent of any known sin that dents our Christian walk with the Lord Jesus Christ.

Apostle Paul had this to say:

*I find then a law, that, when I would do good,
evil is present with me. For I delight in the
law of God after the inward man: But I see
another law in my members, warring against
the law of my mind, and bringing me into captivity
to the law of sin which is in my members.
O wretched man that I am! who shall deliver me
from the body of this death? I thank God
through Jesus Christ our Lord. So then with
the mind I myself serve the law of God;
but with the flesh the law of sin.*
Romans 7:21-25

The above scripture makes a lot of sin if you examine your own life. Evil is present every time we strive to do good. What shall we say then? Shall we continue in sin, that grace may abound? God forbid. *"How shall we, that are dead to sin, live any longer therein?"* (Romans 6:1-2)

*Examine yourselves, whether ye be in the faith;
prove your own selves. Know ye not your own selves,
how that Jesus Christ is in you, except ye be reprobates?*

2 Corinthians 13:5

Although most faith people live in denial about the work of the flesh, from my own scriptural understanding, everyone operating within the scope of Galatians 5:20-21 is classified as a sinner.

HOW DO I COME OUT OF SIN?

These prevailing, dominating, controlling forces will not casually go away. Unless you're taking actions by faith, those evil forces will continue to remote control your life and destiny.

You must ***REPENT***, ***CONFESS*** and ***PROCLAIM*** the **LORD JESUS CHRIST.**

The word says as many as received him, to them gave He power to become the sons of God. Even to them that believe on his name.

To qualify for divine visitation, do the following (with sincerity):

1) ***Acknowledge*** that you are a sinner and that He died for you. (Romans 3:23)

2) ***Repent of your sins***. (Acts 3:19, Luke 13:5, 2 Peter 3:9)

3) ***Believe in your heart*** that Jesus died for your sin. (Romans 10:10)

4) ***Confess Jesus as the Lord over your life.*** (Romans

10:10, Acts 2:21)

Now repeat this Prayer after me—

Say Lord Jesus, I accept you today, as my Lord and my savior, forgive me of my sins wash me with your blood. Right now, I believe, I am sanctified, I am save, I am free, I am free from the Power of sin to serve the Lord Jesus. Thank you Lord for saving me. Amen.

Congratulations.

YOU ARE NOW A BORN AGAIN CHRISTIAN!

First of all, you must believe that there is a Holy Spirit.

1) *Acknowledge* the person of the Holy Spirt.

2) *Believe* in the ministration of the Holy Spirit

3) *Submit and obey* the person of the Holy Spirit.

4) *Welcome* the sweet presence of the Holy Spirit.

SUMMARY OF CHAPTER ONE

—We all have great destiny that we must work tirelessly to fulfil in our lifetime.

—We are absolutely responsible for the outcome of our lives.

—Life will only deliver to you what you fight for.

—If you fold your hand, you will frustrate the gift and calling of God over our lives.

—We must be determined to be successful in life.

—We must be disciplined to be successful in life.

—We must be dedicated to make an impact in our lifetime.

—We must make personal efforts by working hard and learning from failure.

—Excellence is not an exception, it is a prevailing attitude.

Chapter 1 How Do I Restore My Destiny?

DECISION KEYS

1) Nothing changes until you make up your mind.

2) Decision is the gateway to deliverance.

3) Until you decide, no one will decide for you.

4) Your prosperity is proportional to your decisions.

5) The decision you make will determine the future you will create

6) Decision creates future and fulfills destinies.

7) Decision beautifies our future.

8) Decision keeps you out of trouble.

9) Decision exempts you from evil.

10) Decision gurantees eternity.

11) You can only go far in life by your faith decisions.

12) You are poor because you made such decisions

13) Make a decision and change your life.

14) Life changing decisions are a function of quality

information.

15) Success in life is a function of decision.

16) Life experiences are full of decisions.

17) Decisions change destinies.

18) Never settle for information—always look for revelation.

19) You are where you are today based on your last decision.

20) Information is crucial in decision making.

21) Decision makers rule the world.

22) You can rule your world with quality decisions.

23) As long as you decide righteously, Satan cannot harrass you.

CHAPTER 2

RECOGNIZING YOUR TALENT

For the gifts and calling of God are without repentance.
Romans 11:29

We are all called by God with diversity of gifts. The Bible says many are called but few are chosen. As believers, we must be able to recognize our talents from a very young age.

For I would that all men were even as I myself.
But every man hath his proper gift of God,
one after this manner, and another after that.
1 Corinthians 7:7

But as God hath distributed to every man,
as the Lord hath called every one, so let him walk.
And so ordain I in all churches.
1 Corinthians 7:17

Let every man abide in the same calling
wherein he was called.
1 Corinthians 7:20

Brethren, let every man, wherein he is called,
therein abide with God.
1 Corinthians 7:24

With the above scriptures in mind, you will appreciate that we are all called in different areas of discipline. We must therefore identify our area of calling and work towards it in our lifetime.

HOW DO I FULFILL MY CALLING IN LIFE?

We must first discover our calling in life

We must take conscious inventory of our lives and tell ourselves the truth. There is something you are very good at. Perhaps it's sports or running or jumping or singing. You are absolutely responsible to discover it and to work towards it in your lifetime.

Have faith in your abilities and have faith in God

For our glorious destiny to flourish, we must have faith in God and in our individual abilities to accomplish greater tasks. It is written that without faith you cannot please God. Remember, Jesus said have faith in God.

Let the world know you by your work

"Brethren, I count not myself to have apprehended: but this one thing I do, forgetting those things which are behind, and reaching forth unto those things which are before, I press toward the mark for the prize of the high calling of God in Christ Jesus." (Philippians 3:13-14)

Always seek for mentors to follow their path

"Thus saith the Lord, Stand ye in the ways, and see, and ask for the old paths, where is the good way, and walk therein, and ye shall find rest for your souls. But they said, We will not walk therein." (Jeremiah 6:16)

Whatever is your heart's desire, someone has done it before. Mentors are the shortcut to breakthrough. Without mentors, we are left to the tormentor. We must all seek for mentors in any area of life we find ourselves. *"That ye be not slothful, but followers of them who through faith and patience inherit the promises."* (Hebrews 6:12)

Asa Alonso Allen (March 27, 1911 – June 11, 1970), better known as A. A. Allen, was a minister with a Pentecostal evangelistic healing and deliverance ministry. He was, for a time, associated with the "Voice of Healing" movement founded by Gordon Lindsay. This great evangelist followed his mentors—the great D.L. Moody and Charles Finney. His first preaching message was a combination of two sermons from these two great men of God.

Benefits of a Mentor

—Mentors bring out the best of us. As long as you have a mentor, it is not easy for you to fail. Mentors develop our inner strength and bring out the best in our talents.

—Mentors help us eliminate mistakes in life. We correct our lives in any area where our mentors failed.

—Mentors grant us the assurance and confidence that we will succeed in our area of calling.

—Mentors help us reduce risk in life. Whatever hindered and destroyed your mentor can easily be overcome because you already have some information.

—Mentors help us shape and fulfil our destiny and calling in Christ. Mentors help shape our future. May you discover your mentor today and follow their teaching diligently.

—Mentors help us eliminate weaknesses. As long as you follow a mentor, your weaknesses will be pruned as you continue to learn from your mentor.

—Our mentor helps encourage us in our area of discipline in life.

PRAYER POINT

—Let frustration and disappointment be the portion of every object fashioned against my life and family, in the name of Jesus.

—Break every tie to polluted objects and items between my life and family, in the name of Jesus.

—Break every unspoken curse against my life, in the name of Jesus.

—Break every curse pronounced inwardly against my destiny, in the name of Jesus.

—Break you inward curses militating against my virtues, break, in the name of Jesus.

—Summersault and die every power given the mandate to curse and hinder my progress, in the mighty name of Jesus.

—Fall down and die every spirit of Balaam hired to curse my progress, in the name of Jesus.

—Break by fire every curse that I have brought into my life through ignorance and disobedience, in the name of Jesus.

—Every power magnetizing physical and spiritual curses to me, I raise the blood of Jesus against you and I challenge you by fire, in the name of Jesus.

—Father, Lord, turn all my self-imposed curses to blessings, in the name of Jesus.

—Every instrument, put in place to frustrate me from becoming impotent, in the name of Jesus.

—I reject every cycle of frustration, in the mighty name of Jesus.

—Perish by fire every agent assigned to frustrate me, in the name of Jesus.

—Die by the sword every power tormenting Nigeria, in the name of Jesus.

—I destroy the power of every satanic arrest in my life, in the name of Jesus.

—All satanic-arresting agents, release me in the mighty name of our Lord Jesus Christ.

—Everything that is representing me in the demonic world against my career, be destroyed by the fire of God, in the name of Jesus.

—Spirit of the living God, quicken the whole of my being, in the name of Jesus.

—God, smash me and renew my strength, in the mighty name of Jesus.

—Holy Spirit, open my eyes to see beyond the visible to the invisible, in the name of Jesus.

—Lord, ignite my career with Your fire.

—O Lord, liberate my spirit to follow the leading of the Holy Spirit.

—Holy Spirit, teach me to pray *through* problems instead of praying *about* problems, in the name of Jesus.

—O Lord, deliver me from the lies I tell myself.

—Be roasted every evil spiritual padlock and evil chain hindering my success, in the name of Jesus.

—I rebuke every spirit of spiritual deafness and blindness in my life, in the name of Jesus.

—O Lord, empower me to resist satan that he would flee, in the name of Jesus.

—I chose to believe the report of the Lord and no other, in the name of Jesus.

—Lord, anoint my eyes and my ears that they may see and hear wondrous things from heaven.

—O Lord, anoint me to pray without ceasing.

—In the name of Jesus, I capture every power behind any career failure.

—Holy Spirit, rain on me now, in the name of Jesus.

—Holy Spirit, uncover my darkest secrets, in the name of Jesus.

—You spirit of confusion, lose your hold over my life, in the name of Jesus.

—In the power of the Holy Spirit, I defy satan's power upon my career, in the name of Jesus.

—Let water of life flush out every unwanted stranger in my life, in the name of Jesus.

—You the enemies of my career, be paralyzed, in the name of Jesus.

—O Lord, begin to clean away from my life all that does not reflect You.

—Holy Spirit fire, ignite me to the glory of God, in the name of Jesus.

—Oh Lord, let the anointing of the Holy Spirit break every yoke of backwardness in my life.

—I frustrate every demonic arrest over my spirit-man, in the name of Jesus.

—Let the blood of Jesus remove any unprogressive label from every aspect of my life, in Jesus' name.

—Be revoked anti-breakthrough decrees, in the name of Jesus.

—Holy Ghost fire, destroy every satanic garments in my life, in the name of Jesus

CHAPTER 3

THE POWER OF MENTORSHIP

That ye be not slothful, but followers of them who through faith and patience inherit the promises.
Hebrews 6:12

Mentors and coaches are designed by God to produce the best in us. These are men and women who have gone ahead of us, seen ahead of us and foretell us of the future ahead. As a businessman, a professor, a soccer footballer and a preacher, we all need a mentor.

My mentors—like the late Oral Roberts, Keneth Hagin, A.A. Allen, T.L. Osborne—gave me the confidence from their books and life that I will do well in ministry, if I'm able to adhere to their teachings and books. Mentors give us shortcuts to our breakthroughs in life. Elijah mentored Elisha. Elijah performed 16 miracles in his lifetime, but Elisha, his mentee, performed 32 miracles in his lifetime. *"And it came to pass, when they were gone over, that Elijah said unto Elisha, Ask what I shall do for thee, before I be taken away from thee. And Elisha said, I pray thee, let a double portion of thy spirit be upon me."* (2 Kings 2:9)

Mentors are channels to express old truths in a new way. John the Baptist, who mentored Jesus, preached the baptism of repentance for the remission of our sins. But Jesus came to express this old truth in a new way by preaching love, grace and truth.

Thus saith the Lord, Stand ye in the ways, and see, and ask for the old paths, where is the good way, and walk therein, and ye shall find rest for your souls. But they said, We will not walk therein.
Jeremiah 6:16

WITHOUT MENTORS WE ARE LEFT TO THE TORMENTOR

For us to grow in the knowledge of the truth and be established, we must embrace the concept of a mentor in our lives. Some folks tell me, " I do not need a mentor, I read some books." The truth is, somebody wrote those books you read and got knowledge from.

HINDRACE TO MENTORSHIP

PRIDE & ARROGANCY

The Bible says that pride goeth before destruction. *"Pride goeth before destruction, and an haughty spirit before a fall."* (Proverbs 16:18) In my understanding, we all need a mentor and a coach in our lifetime. Even Jesus needed John the Baptist to baptize him.

DISOBEDIENT

But if ye refuse and rebel, ye shall be devoured with the sword: for the mouth of the Lord hath spoken it.
Isaiah 1:20

All stubborn and disobedient people will never accept the concept of a mentor. But as long as you are living in disobedience you will always suffer frustration because of lack of a mentor and a coach in your life.

UNWILLING TO LEARN
Some of us will never learn from nobody, because we lack the spirit to learn from anybody. An unwilling spirit to learn will hinder us from mentorship. And as long as we are not open to learning, to embrace ideas from experienced people, we will never grow in life.

ACCESS INTO THE SUPERNATURAL

BE BORN AGAIN
We must be born again for us to experience the supernatural and mentorship.

*Jesus answered and said unto him, Verily, verily,
I say unto thee, Except a man be born again,
he cannot see the kingdom of God. Nicodemus saith
unto him, How can a man be born when he is old?
can he enter the second time into his mother's womb,
and be born? Jesus answered, Verily, verily, I say unto
thee, Except a man be born of water and of the Spirit,
he cannot enter into the kingdom of God.
That which is born of the flesh is flesh; and that which
is born of the Spirit is spirit. Marvel not that I said unto
thee, Ye must be born again. The wind bloweth where
it listeth, and thou hearest the sound thereof, but canst
not tell whence it cometh, and whither it goeth: so is
every one that is born of the Spirit.*
John 3:3-8

We must therefore obey the voice of the Lord, confess him as Lord and savior, then we can learn from His teaching and position our lives to encounter the supernatural.

THE FEAR OF GOD

One of the greatest channels to position our lives to encounter the supernatural is to covet the spirit of the fear of God. *"The fear of the Lord is the beginning of wisdom: and the knowledge of the holy is understanding."* (Proverbs 9:10)

RIGHTEOUS LIFESTYLE

It may take a longer time, but over the course of your lifetime it will show. Righteousness is a virtue that tells everybody around you the way you live, the way you do business and the way you operate. *"For the vision is yet for an appointed time, but at the end it shall speak, and not lie: though it tarry, wait for it; because it will surely come, it will not tarry."* (Habakkuk 2:3)

INTEGRITY

The integrity of the upright shall guide them.
Proverbs 11:3

As long as you carry integrity in your heart, it will guide your life from all assaults and attacks of the devil. *"So he fed them according to the integrity of his heart; and guided them by the skillfulness of his hands."* (Psalms 78:72)

AGREEMENT

Until you agree with the Holy Spirit by believing God's word to be true, you will forever suffer frustration. Once you agree with the Holy Spirit, you are guaranteed access into the supernatural. *"Again I say unto you, That if two of you shall agree on Earth as touching any thing that they shall ask, it shall be done for them of my Father which is in heaven."* (Matthew 18:19)

"For where two or three are gathered together in my name, there am I in the midst of them." (Matthew 18:20)

Remember... *"The Lord thy God in the midst of thee is mighty."* (Zephaniah 3:17)

SOUL WINNING

It is written, *"And he that winneth souls is wise."* (Proverbs 11:30) Soul winning is the gateway into the supernatural. As long as you win souls for Jesus, he will decorate your life and destiny.

PRINCIPLES OF DIVINE CONNECTION

—Have faith in God.
—Believe in yourself.
—Always follow the footsteps of your mentors.
—Always carry a mental picture of your actual future.
—Live a righteous life.
—Keep company with the right people.
—Be willing to confront all your challenges/conflicts.
—Never give up in life.
—Be disciplined.
—Be dedicated.
—Be determined.
—Always make personal efforts and sacrifice.
—Depart from evil and learn to do well.

CONCLUSION

And I will restore to you the years that the locust hath eaten, the cankerworm, and the caterpiller, and the palmerworm, my great army which I sent among you.
Joel 2:25

Irrespective of how far you have gone in a wrong direction, you will never get to the destination. We are all called by God, but few are chosen. *"For many are called, but few are chosen."* (Matthew 22:14)

*Wherefore the rather, brethren,
give diligence to make your calling and election sure:
for if ye do these things, ye shall never fall.*
2 Peter 1:9

*Who hath saved us, and called us with an holy calling,
not according to our works, but according to
his own purpose and grace, which was given us
in Christ Jesus before the world began.*
2 Timothy 1:10

Without purpose your life has no meaning. Every career is not for you, but there IS an assignment for your life.

For I would that all men were even as I myself.
But every man hath his proper gift of God,
one after this manner, and another after that.
1 Corinthians 7:7
But as God hath distributed to every man,
as the Lord hath called every one, so let him walk.
And so ordain I in all churches.
1 Corinthians 7:17

Let every man abide in the same calling
wherein he was called.
1 Corinthians 7:20

Brethren, let every man, wherein he is called,
therein abide with God.
1 Corinthians 7:24

God is willing to restore our lives, but you have a part to play in this relationship.

HAVE YOU DISCOVERED YOUR GIFT FROM GOD?

A man's gift maketh room for him,
and bringeth him before great men.
Proverbs 18:16

Although God wants you to breakthrough in life, you have a greater role to play in this covenant relationship. Remember how Joseph's gift in the Bible brought him before the king? Daniel's gift in the Bible brought him before four presidents and kings.

Discover your talent from God and pursue it with all your might. You must recover your destiny in the mighty name of Jesus. Don't give up on your destiny because winners do not quit. Never waste any day of your life because your time is your money.

FAVOR CONFESSION

Father, thank you for making me righteous and accepted through the blood of Jesus Christ. Because of that, I am blessed and highly favored by God. I am the subject of your affection. Your favor surrounds me as a shield, and the first thing that people see around me is your favored shield.

Thank you that I have favor with you and man today. All day long people go out of their way to bless me and help me. I have favor with everyone that I deal with today. Doors that were once closed are now opened for me. I receive preferential treatment and I have special privileges. I am God's favored child.

No good thing will He withhold from me. Because of God's favor, my enemies cannot triumph over my life. I have supernatural increases and promotions. I declare restoration to everything that the devil has stolen from my life. I have honor in the midst of my adversaries and an increase in assets, especially in real estate and expansion of territories.

Because I am highly favored by God, I experience great victories, supernatural turnarounds and miraculous breakthroughs in the midst of great impossibilities. I receive recognition, prominence and honor. Petitions are granted to me even by ungodly authorities. Policies, rules, regulations and laws are changed and reversed on my behalf.

I win battles that I don't even have to fight, because God fights them for me. This is the day, the set time and the designated moment for me to experience the free favor of God that profusely and lavishly abounds on my behalf, in Jesus' name. Amen.

YOU MUST BE BORN AGAIN

If you are a born again Christian, we'd like to encourage you in your Christian life. If you are not a born again Christian, we can help you here receive genuine salvation. *"Therefore if any man be in Christ, he is a new creature: old things are passed away; behold, all things are become new."* (2 Corinthians 5:17)

Now repeat this prayer after me:

Say Lord Jesus, I accept you today, as my Lord and my savior, forgive me of my sins, wash me with your blood. Right now I believe, I am sanctified, I am saved, I am free, I am free from the power of sin to serve the Lord Jesus. Thank you, Lord, for saving me. Amen.

Congratulations...

YOU ARE NOW A BORN AGAIN CHRISTIAN!
WHAT MUST I DO TO DETERMINE MY DIVINE VISITATION?

To determine divine visitation you must be born again!

The Word says as many as received him, to them gave He power to become the sons of God. Even to them that believe on His name. To qualify for divine visitation, do the following sincerely:

1) Acknowledge that you are a sinner and that He died for you. (Romans 3:23)

2) Repent of your sins. (Acts 3:19, Luke 13:5, 2 Peter 3:9)

3) Believe in your heart that Jesus died for your sin. (Romans 10:10)

4) Confess Jesus as the Lord over your life. (Romans 10:10, Acts 2:21)

Now repeat this prayer after me:

"Say Lord Jesus, I accept you today, as my Lord and my savior, forgive me of my sins, wash me with your blood. Right now, I believe, I am sanctified, I am saved, I am free, I am free from the power of sin to serve the Lord Jesus.
Thank you Lord for saving me. Amen."
Congratulations.

YOU ARE NOW A BORN AGAIN CHRISTIAN!

AGAIN I SAY TO YOU...

CONGRATULATIONS!

I adjure you to watch the Spirit of God bearing witness, with your Spirit confirming His word with signs. The Word says the Spirit itself beareth witness with our spirit, that we are the children of God. Join a Bible-believing church—or join us for our weekly and Sunday worship services at 343 Sanford Avenue, Newark, New Jersey 07106.

WISDOM KEYS

—Every productive society is a society heading to the top.

—Millions of Nigerians run away from Nigeria. Very few Nigerians stay in Nigeria.

—My decision to return Nigeria is the will of God for my life.

—My shortcoming in America after 18 years is the fact that I've trained me to be wise, to think, reflect and reason appropriately.

—If you train your mind to reason, it will train your hands to earn money.

—It is absurd to use the money of the heathen to build the kingdom of the living God.

—Every ministry reveals its agenda and VISION either at the beginning or at the end.

—Be careful of your life. It is your first ministry.

—The average American mind is conditioned for a continual quest to get new things and discard the old.

—When I considered well, my BMW jeep became my initial deposit for the work of the ministry in Nigeria.

—Money will never fall from any tree or person. Make up your mind to be independent today.

—Everyone is waiting for you to change your mind. Until you change your thinking, nothing changes around you.

—Multiple academic degrees in other disciplines gave me the chance to think and reason.

—Whatever anyone is thinking at any time reveals what is inside of their heart.

—All planned events are the product of meditation.

—Every event is designed for a designated timeline.

—Wisdom is your ability to think, to create and invent.

— If you can think wisely enough, you will come out of debt.

—The distance between you and your success is your innovative and creative ability to think well.

—Success is the result of hard work, commitment, resolve and determined learning from past mistakes and failings.

—If you organize your mind, you have organized your

life and destiny.

—There is a thin line between success and failure.

—Wealth is your ability to think, power is your ability to reason and success is your ability to be informed.

—If you can make use of your mind by thinking and reasoning, God will make use of your life and destiny.

—Reflect, reason, think and be great.

—Famous people are born of woman.

—That you will make it is your intention, that you will survive is your resolve, that you will succeed with changes is your determination, personal efforts and hard work.

—No man was born a failure.

—Lack of vision is the result of failure.

—Working with mental patients encourages and aspire me to be a productive observant and dedicated to my assignment.

—Successful people are not magicians. It is the will-power, combined with hard work and determination and a resolve to succeed, that make them succeed.

—In the unequivocal state of the mind, intention is not a location or a position. It is the state of the mind.

—So many people think that they think. The mind is used to think, to reflect and to reason. You will remain blind with your eyes open until you can see with your mind by thinking.

—There is no favoritism in accurate and precise calculation.

—Although knowledge is power, information is the key and gateway to a great future.

—It will take the hand of God to move the hand of man.

—With the backing of the great wise God, nothing will disconnect you from your inheritance.

—As long as you have wisdom and understanding of God, Satan and evil cannot manipulate your life and destiny.

—You have come this far in life by your own judgment and the decisions you made in the past. Now lean in and listen to God for another dimension of greatness.

—Great people are ordinary people. It is extra ordinary efforts and the price of sacrifice that produces greatness in them.

—As a mental direct care worker, I saw a great pastor and a motivational speaker within myself.

—A menial job does not reduce your self-worth. Until you resolve to achieve greatness and see greatness in all you do, you will never count in your community.

—The principle of Jesus will solve your gambling and addiction problems.

—The man of Jesus will lead you into heaven.

—Everyone has their self-appraisal and what they think about you. Until you discover yourself, other opinions about you will alter the real you.

—Supervisors and directors are just a position in the chain of command in a workplace. Never allow your supervisor hierarchy to alter your opinion of yourself.

—Everyone can come out of debt if they make up their mind.

—The fact that I am not a decision-maker at work does not diminish my contribution to my world.

—Although it appears like it was a poor decision to accept a direct care employment at a psychiatric hospital, as I reflect on my nine years of that experience, it became apparent that I have learned and experienced enough for my next assignment.

—Self-encouragement and determination is a resolve of the heart.

—If you are determined to make a difference and do the things that make a difference, you will eventually make a difference.

—Good things do not come easy.

—Short cuts will cut your life short.

—Those who look ahead move ahead.

—Life is all about making an impact. In your lifetime strive to make an impact in your community.

—Make friends and connect with people who are moving ahead of you in life.

—If you can look around well, you have come a long way in your life, made a lot of difference and realized a lot of success in life.

—If you are my old friend, hurry up to reach out to me before I become a stranger to you.

—I am blessed with inspirations from God that changed my interpretation of the world around me.

—I thought I was stagnant and lonely until I looked around and noticed my children running around and my wife cooking.

—At 40, I resigned my job to seek the Lord forever.

—My ministry took a drastic rise to the top when the wisdom of God visited me with knowledge and understanding.

—You will be a better person if you understand the characteristics of your personality like your mood swings, attitudes and habits.

—It is the seed of love you sow into the heart of a child and a woman that you reap in due time.

—Love is not selfish. Love shares everything, including the concealed secrets of the mind.

—As long as you have a prayer life and a Bible, you will never feel lonely in the race of life.

—When good friends disconnect from you, let them go. They might have seen something new in a different direction.

—Confidence in yourself and in God is the only way to bring you out of captivity

—Never train a child to waste his or her time.

—The mind is the greatest asset of a great future.

—You walk by common sense, run by principles and fly by instruction.

—Those who become successful in life did it by self-determination, hard work and learning from past failures.

—Most successful people are lonely people. No one renders help to them, believing they are already successful. Except when they seek for more knowledge and information, they are all alone.

— I have seen a towing truck vehicle. I have also seen a towing ship in the water. But I have never seen a towing airplane in the air.

—I exercise my judgment and make a decision every minute of the day. Decisions are crucial, critical and vital with reference to your future.

—So many people wish for a great future. You can only work towards a great future.

—Your celebrity status began when you discovered

your talent. What are you good at? Work at it with all your commitment.

—Prayers will sustain you, but the wisdom of God will prosper you.

—When I met Oyedepo, his teachings changed my perspective. But when I met Ibiyeomie, his teachings changed my perception.

—I will be successful in ministry if only I concentrate and focus my energy in the work of the ministry.

—It took the late Dr. Norman Vincent Peale's book to open my mind towards the kingdom of success.

CHAPTER 4

PRAYER OF SALVATION

It will profit us nothing as a ministry if, after reading this book, your salvation is still questionable. I long to see you saved and delivered from all the wiles and schemes of the devil.

ARE YOU SAVED?

The honest truth is, the Lord Jesus really does not know you unless you are saved. For as many as are led by the Spirit of God, they are the sons of God. *"For ye have not received the spirit of bondage again to fear; but ye have received the Spirit of adoption, whereby we cry, Abba, Father. The Spirit itself beareth witness with our spirit, that we are the children of God."* (Romans 8:14-16)

What must I do to determine my divine visitation?

To determine divine visitation, you must be born again!

The Word says as many as received him, to them gave He power to become the sons of God. Even to them that believe on his name.

To qualify for divine visitation, do the following with sincerity—

> 1) Acknowledge that you are a sinner and that He died for you. (Romans 3:23)
>
> 2) Repent of your sins. (Acts 3:19, Luke 13:5, 2 Peter 3:9)
>
> 3) Believe in your heart that Jesus died for your sins. (Romans 10:10)
>
> 4) Confess Jesus as the Lord over your life. (Romans 10:10, Acts 2:21)

Now repeat this prayer after me:

Say Lord Jesus, I accept you today, as my Lord and my savior. Forgive me of my sins, wash me with your blood. Right now, I believe I am sanctified, I am saved, I am free. I am free from the power of sin, to serve the Lord Jesus. Thank you Lord for saving me. Amen.

Congratulations. You are now...

A BORN AGAIN CHRISTIAN.

Again I say to you—CONGRATULATIONS!

I adjure you to watch the Spirit of God bear witness with your Spirit, confirming His word with subsequent signs. The word says, *"The Spirit itself beareth witness with our spirit, that we are the children of God."* (Romans 8:16)

MIRACLE CARE OUTREACH

"...But that the members should have the same care one for another"
1 Corinthians 12:25

We are all members of the body of Christ. Jesus commanded us to love our neighbor as ourselves. This includes caring for one another as a member of one body. True love is expressed in caring and giving. The word says, for God so Love He gave....

Reach out to someone in need of Jesus. Help someone in crisis find Christ. Look out and prove your love to Jesus by caring and inviting your friends and associates to find Jesus the Healer.

Invite your friends to our Home Care Cell Fellowship (Miracle Chapel Intl. Satellite Fellowship). We're in the U.S. at 33 Schley Street, Newark, New Jersey 07112. Home Care Cell Fellowship Group meets every Tuesday at 6:00pm-7:00pm.

If you are in Nigeria—MIRACLE OF GOD MINISTRIES, aka "MIRACLE CHAPEL INTL."

Mpama–Egbu-Owerri Imo state Nigeria.

LIFE IS NOT ALL ABOUT DURATION, BUT IT'S ALL ABOUT DONATION

What does this statement mean?

Life consists not in accumulation of material wealth.
Luke 12:15

But it's all about liberality…meaning, what you can give and share with others. *"When you live for others—You live forever"* (Proverbs 11:25) because you outlive your generation by the legacy you live behind after you depart into glory to be with the Lord. But when you live to yourself - you are reduced to self— you are easily forgotten when you die and depart in glory. Permit me to admonish you today to live your life to be a blessing to a soul connected to you today. I want you to know that so many souls are connected and looking up to you, and through you so many souls will be saved and rescued from destruction. Will you disciple someone today to find Jesus Christ?

As a genuine Christian, it is your duty to evangelize Jesus Christ to all you meet on your way. Jesus is still in the healing business-Jesus is still doing miracles from time of old to now. Therefore tell someone about Jesus Christ today, disciple and bring them to Church.

Philip findeth Nathanael…
John 1:45

Please to prove the sincerity of your love for God today; please become a soul winner. The dignity of your Christianity is hidden in your boldness to proclaim and evangelize Jesus Christ to all you meet on your way. There is a question mark on the integrity of your Christianity until you become a life soul winner. Invite someone to join us worship the Lord Jesus this coming Sunday. Amen.

MIRACLE OF GOD MINISTRIES

PILLARS OF THE COMMISSION

We Believe, Preach and Practice the following:

1) We believe and preach Salvation to every living human being.

2) We believe and preach Repentance and Forgiveness of sins.

3) We believe and preach the baptism of the Holy Spirit and Spiritual gifts.

4) We believe and teach Prosperity.

5) We believe and preach Divine Healing and Miracles—Signs and Wonder.

6) We believe and preach Faith.

7) We believe and proclaim the Power of God (Supernatural).

8) We believe and proclaim Praise and Worship to God.

9) We believe and preach Wisdom.

10) We believe and preach Holiness (Consecration).

11) We believe and preach Vision.

12) We believe and teach the Word of God.

13) We believe and teach Success.

14) We believe and practice Prayer.

15) We believe and teach Deliverance.

These 15 stones form the Pillars of Our Commission. Become part of this church family and follow this great move of God.

MY HEARTFELT PRAYER FOR YOU

It is my prayer that you testify today about the goodness of the Lord. I desire for you to have an encounter with our Lord Jesus Christ.

Now let me pray for you:

Heavenly Father, may today be a day of new beginnings for this precious loved one. Lord God of heaven, open a new chapter in the life of this precious loved one reading this book today. May all their secret prayers be answered in the mighty name of Jesus. We thank you Jesus for hearing us. In Jesus' mighty name. Amen.

ETERNITY IS REAL

It will profit us nothing as a ministry if you finish reading this book without making plans for heaven. You must make conscious plans to make heaven because eternity is real.

Indeed, we live in an immoral time. Sin has gained so much ground and promotion that even the righteous are tempted to fall short of the glory of God.

You might ask me, what must I do to be saved?

As long as we believe and repent, God is willing to forgive and to restore our lives. *"And they said, Believe on the Lord Jesus Christ, and thou shalt be saved, and thy house."* (Acts 16:31)

Salvation is possible only through the name of our Lord Jesus Christ. *"Neither is there salvation in any other: for there is none other name under heaven given among men, whereby we must be saved."* (Acts 4:12)

I admonish you, therefore, to think twice before you commit those sins that not only easily beset you, but also separate you far away from God. As long as you repent even now, God is more than willing to restore and save your life from eternal hellfire. *"And make straight paths for your feet, lest that which is lame be turned out of the way; but let it rather be healed. Follow peace with all men, and holiness, without which no man shall see the Lord."* (Hebrews 12:13-14)

Make conscious plans to make heaven. Change the way you approach things and God will restore and forgive you of all your sins. Amen

CHAPTER 5

ABOUT THE AUTHOR

Rev. Franklin N. Abazie is the founding and Presiding Pastor of Miracle of God Ministries, with headquarters in Newark, New Jersey USA and a branch church in Owerri-Imo State Nigeria. He is following the footsteps of one of his mentors, the healing evangelist Oral Roberts of the blessed memory. The Lord passed Oral Roberts' healing mantle two days before he went to be with the Lord at age 91 into the hands of healing evangelist Rev. Franklin N. Abazie in a vision.

In all his services, the Power and Presence of God is present to heal all in his audience. Rev. Abazie is an ordained man of God, with a Healing Ministry reviving the healing and miracle ministry of Jesus Christ of Nazareth.

Pastor Franklin N. Abazie, has been called by God with a unique mandate: **"THE MOMENT IS DUE TO IMPACT YOUR WORLD THROUGH THE REVIVAL OF THE HEALING AND MIRACLE MINISTRY OF JESUS CHRIST OF NAZARETH.**

"I AM SENDING YOU TO RESTORE HEALTH UNTO THEE AND I WILL HEAL THEE OF THY WOUNDS, SAID THE LORD OF HOST."

Rev. Abazie is a gifted, ardent teacher of the word of God, who operates also in the office of a Prophet, generating and attracting undeniable signs and wonders, special miracles and healings, with apostolic fireworks of the Holy Ghost. He is the founding and presiding senior Pastor of this fast growing Healing Ministry. He has written over 86 inspirational, healing and transforming books covering almost all aspects of divine healing and life. He is happily married and blessed with children.

BOOKS BY REV. FRANKLIN N. ABAZIE:

1) The Outcome of Faith
2) Understanding the Secret of Prevailing Prayers
3) Commanding Abundance
4) Understanding the Secret of the Man God Uses
5) Activating My Due Season
6) Overcoming Divine Verdicts
7) The Outcome of Divine Wisdom
8) Understanding God's Restoration Mandate
9) Walking In the Victory and Authority of the Truth
10) God's Covenant Exemption
11) Destiny Restoration Pillars
12) Provoking Acceptable Praise
13) Understanding Divine Judgment
14) Activating Angelic Re-enforcement
15) Provoking Un-Merited Favo
16) The Benefits of the Speaking Faith
17) Understanding Divine Arrangement
18) How to Keep Your Healing
19) Understanding the Mysteries of the Speaking Faith
20) Understanding the Mysteries of Prophetic Healing
21) Operating Under the Rules of Creative Healing
22) Understanding the Joy of Breakthrough
23) Understanding the Mystery of Breakthrough
24) Understanding Divine Prosperity
25) Understanding Divine Healing
26) Retaining Your Inheritance
27) Overcoming Confusing Spirit
28) Commanding Angelic Escorts

29) Enforcing Your Inheritance In Christ Jesus
30) Understanding Your Guardian Angels
31) Overcoming the Dominion of Sin
32) Understanding the Voice of God
33) The Outstanding Benefits of the Anointing
34) The Audacity of the Blood of Jesus
35) Walking in the Reality of the Anointing
36) Escaping the Nightmare of Poverty
37) Understanding Your Harvest Season
38) Activating Your Success Buttons
39) Overcoming the Forces of Darkness
40) Overcoming the Devices of the Devil
41) Overcoming Demonic Agents
42) Overcoming the Sorrows of Failure
43) Rejecting the Sorrows of Failure
44) Resisting the Sorrows of Poverty
45) Restoring Broken Marriages
46) Redeeming Your Days
47) The Force of Vision
48) Overcoming the Forces of Ignorance
49) Understanding the Sacrifice of Small Beginning
50) The Might of Small Beginning
51) Understanding the Mysteries of Prophesy
52) Overcoming Dream Nightmares
53) Breaking the Shackles of the Curse of the Law
54) Understanding the Joy of Harvest
55) Wisdom for Signs & Wonders
56) Wisdom for Generational Impact
57) Wisdom for Marriage Stability
58) Understanding the Number of Your Days

59) Enforcing Your Kingdom Rights
60) Escaping the Traps of Immoralities
61) Escaping the Trap of Poverty
62) Accessing Biblical Prosperity
63) Accessing True Riches in Christ
64) Silencing the Voice of the Accuser
65) Overcoming the Forces of Oppositions
66) Quenching the Voice of the Avenger
67) Silencing Demonic Prediction & Projection
68) Silencing Your Mocker
69) Understanding the Power of the Holy Ghost
70) Understanding the Baptism of Power
71) The Mystery of the Blood of Jesus
72) Understanding the Mystery of Sanctification
73) Understanding the Power of Holiness
74) Understanding the Forces of Purity & Righteousness
75) Activating the Forces of Vengeance
76) Appreciating the Mystery of Restoration
77) Overcoming the Projection & Prediction of the Enemy
78) Engaging the Mystery of the Blood
79) Commanding the Power of the Speaking Faith
80) Uprooting the Forces Against Your Rising
81) Overcoming Mere Success Syndrome
82) Understanding Divine Sentence
83) Understanding the Mystery of Praise
84) Understanding the Author of Faith
85) The Mystery of the Finisher of Faith
86) Attracting Supernatural Favor

MIRACLE OF GOD MINISTRIES
NIGERIA CRUSADE
2012

MIRACLE OF GOD MINISTRIES
NIGERIA CRUSADE 2012

MIRACLE OF GOD MINISTRIES

NIGERIA CRUSADE

2012

MIRACLE OF GOD MINISTRIES

NIGERIA CRUSADE

2012

MIRACLE OF GOD MINISTRIES

NIGERIA CRUSADE 2012

www.ingramcontent.com/pod-product-compliance
Lightning Source LLC
Chambersburg PA
CBHW021447080526
44588CB00009B/724